I0457411

A, B.

Tamarah Rockwood

Bainbridge Island Press

A,

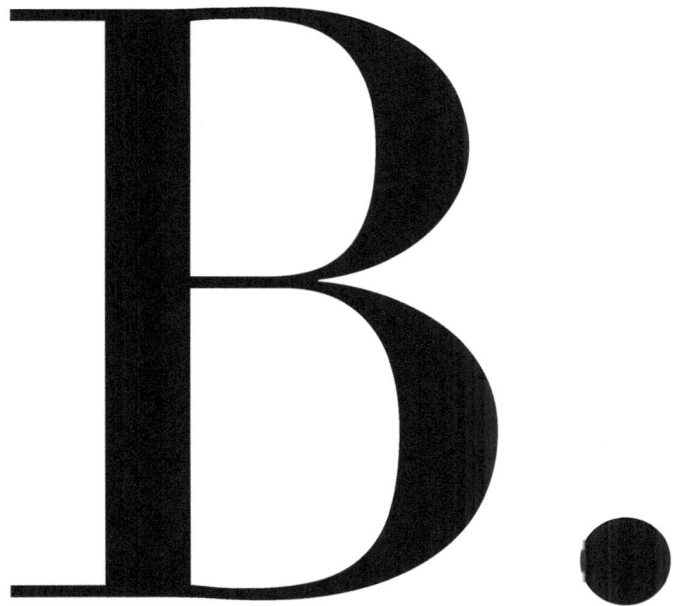

B.

Tamarah Rockwood

Bainbridge Island Press

Bainbridge Island, WA

Bainbridge Island
P R E S S

Copyright ©2023 by Tamarah Rockwood

Published in 2023 by Bainbridge Island Press
Bainbridge Island, WA
https://bainbridgeislandpress.com

All rights reserved.

Printed in the United States of America

ISBN: 978-1-961451-00-1

Library of Congress Control Number: 2023943990

Cover design: Ben Rockwood

9 8 7 6 5 4 3 2

For my children.

Acknowledgements

Greatful acknowledgement is made to the editors of the following journals, anthologies and websites, where version of these poems first appeared:

Oregon Poetry Association (Notable Mention):
    I.

Silence Canbera University International Poetry Award (2019):
    Coyotes Laughing

Livinia Press, Issue 3:
    The Handless Maiden

A Book of Matches (2023):
    8 separate pieces

A Book of Matches (2023):
    The Sex Life of Trees

Poetry Corners (2022), Bainbridge Island Press:
    The Sense of Movement

Paddler Press (2023):
    Cotiere

Table of Contents

Anxiety

Shame

Self

Hope

A, B.

Part I

Anxiety

Overture

Julianne Moore is a private person.
So, we won't talk about her.
We will discuss the stories
of years in my floor:
I look down the long grains
Extending through the wood planks,
Displaying years of droughts and years of rain
And I wonder,
in a thought only for myself,
About the story of the rains,
The stories of the forests and
Which ring held the year when they were sacrificed;
When the ark was built with wood,
Or maybe a sad song.

I.

Speak, girl.
Speak with your tongue.
With these voices you have heard,
Tasted, eaten, spit out, berated,
Joined, feared, admonished,
Grasped and understood-

The voices in the forest
which have raised you
from worm to woman;

Speak, of all
That you have seen
In the keyholes of the canopy:
Of the woodpecker's grit,
Of the coyote's howl,
Of the wasp's territorial nest in the stump,
And of the time when they followed you home and stung you
A thousand times, and how
You killed them all
In the bathroom,

And then

Stood outside on planks of gopherwood,
And stared the forest in its face,
And continued to breathe.
Speak this.

Coyotes Laughing

When the forest changed you
Changed. Its hearty growth
Fell like leaves
And left the floor strewn
With golden intentions of a season.

Verdant pedantic bodies of trees stiff
With buds, clinging to the sheets of dawn;
Hanging impotent and unseeded.
We listened to the vinyl record of jazz
From the night before. Some Davis number.
We both recognized the trumpet
Calling the band out of the woods.

Your arms cast a shadow
Across my face.
I could hear your voice.

It was a voice which spoke through
the waters withheld from Ham.
Designed to carry him away from
The edges of the garden which
Knew him.

In the forest I could hear
The voices dancing around the coyote,
The laughing scoundrel;
They were beautiful, long and full of vines.
Naturally, he drank of their fragrant wine-
Kisses, laid upon him by
Oiled fingers who touched his chest
And anointed him with
The sweat of Gader'el,
Leading his steps into the deep forest
And carving his name
Into the divided branches of the
Tamarisk tree at Gibreah.

We watched the coyote nip
The edge of my garment.

The forest changed, and I
Changed; even though I brought
a hammer to nail into the
Gopherwood.

The Rocks of Yuba

One summer we floated down
The Yuba river on delphic Sav-On
Rafts with old black masks and
Black snorkels rimmed with
Neon orange bands, as if warning
The newly hatched brown trout
That our stuffed mouths were busy
Breathing and not chewing, when
We found something hidden
Underneath a smooth slab of granite, something
Stuck between the crushing stones,
Something waving, patiently after the
Pine flotsam that coursed past
Their brilliantly knotted hook attached
To fine goose down and dyed green
To boast its own difference,
Its incredible agency amongst the dumb
Rocks which held it in place
The rocks which kept it from
Ever flying, from ever ascending
Above the rocks of Yuba;
The river which did not rise too high;
The river of parturition.

A Whiff

Sometimes it only takes that whiff
Of perspective through the dark
Like through a long underground pipe
So that the incense of the world can be smelled
Which, moments ago, seemed so distant and
Angry because the fragrance of feet and
Bodies and flickering tongues behind
Champing teeth when someone says
A word that is packet heavy with Ts,
like intermittent, antiterrorist,
Or antilatitudinarian.

Dandelions

What is it, even?
This fistful of dandelions she brings to me,
fresh picked and golden, held in my face
with earnest meaning in her eyes.

I wonder, are the flowers things of the earth,
a vanitas in this child's plump fingers,
or are the petals a thousand
nonage wishes?

The color of yellow, even,
has no answer for our soul:
Is it cheerful? Are the flowers intelligent?
Do we hold a fistful of cowardice?

Is this nosegay the memory I keep
in the winter of my life, when I remember
my daughters as they were,
and not adults who arrange blankets on my feet?

 If I were a child, I suppose
they would be the entirety of myself,
quick to love and quick to smile;
and my feet would run me across the grass for more.

Reality is, I know, that the dandelions will die
in my pocket, wilted and crushed between
my keys and my wallet;
my quiet memento mori I will find again
In the pocket of winter.

Telling the Bees

When is it time to leave? Is it when
you have looked cleverly at your wrist
waiting with impatient beats of anxiety and
pretending that you have somewhere else to go,
or when you have become bored with
The conversation that bites and politely

Excuse yourself to refresh your drink;
Is it when the words get out of hand after dark,
Or when your heart did not win,
Or when you feel
Like no one has heard one damn thing you've said
And you stare at a freckle on your hand
For too long?
Or is it when you quietly leave a memo
For the beekeeper to tell the bees
You have left.

There is no tree called gopher wood

Likely, it was pitch
Over the planked wood
That kept the water out
Of the stalls and rooms and
Hallways and away from the
Deck chairs, which were all, also,
Called something else, at the time.

The Handless Maiden

I know, we know we know
  We must focus on the Now;
Focus on the present, and also
  Plan for the future.
For what, we ask? For
  The future, stupid:
For the thread we feel pull
  Us, it is our Ace in the Hole.
Words, we know like siblings,
  Which we hate and we love,
We argue against and for
  Words will reject us, we know
How, they get us, they get us.
  The thread we feel pull, on our tongue
To speak, to push, for purpose, for fun.
The women, there are women
  Everywhere! We must bond,
As women, mustn't we?
  As myriad of waves of ways
Some leading to sisters, some
  Threads spinning off women we know,
We know, we must, mustn't we?
  Love all of ourselves, us she?
Ah, and our failure
  We know.
Don't we suffer from failure?
  Or, do we? Do we know
How to fail, since we can only fail
  Once, maybe a time,
Or are we trying to fail,
  We are trying to win,
  We know. The failure happens when
  We know how to fail again.
I know you know the faces
  Of the world, you know
The Tigris, the hummus, the anise
  The airline seats, the taxi lines
The lines, the lines, the lines
  On sand, on walls, on faces,
On fingers, we know these fingers
  These are my fingers, these are your
Fingers, walking across maps, we know.
We know, I know the papers
  Of shelves, of stands, of nightstands,
You know and now I know

What scribbles in the margins:
You wrote what you know.
I know my voice, I know
  Your ears, we know we know
The sounds of the lips that whisper
  Or spit, we know the sound
Of our voice: we know.
Where the sun
  Also shines and flowers also grow;
Thread your fingers between
  Our chairs, lean near
And we breathe,
  We know.

Self

I am not a tree
That cannot speak.
I am not in the sacred canopy
Able to stand so still
And let birds tip tap on
My arms and pick bugs out of
My hardened skin —

I am soft.

Harsh winds have hurt
In times, before.

I am impatient.

I do not slowly grow amber rings
Which celebrate another year;

No, I pace the floors
And worry about the state of
My face before guests arrive.

I am not a tree

Who claims to be sinless.
I know where lies the hornets nest in
The woods, in the stump,
Itching to strike
At bastards who annoy me.

I am not comforted by calm skies
Which do not shake my house and water
My gardens and do not whip
My hair.

The trees standing by my house
Sway together in the wind
That gusts their boughs

As a breath
And sound like they are talking,
Discussing, perhaps, unspoken things.

A Date with Food

I remember the first date we had
When we were very young
And had saved up all of our money
For this dinner out.
We ate only foods
That were drenched in garlic;
Don't ask me why,
We were young and ate the food we loved.

8 separate pieces

I sat in the smaller teal Adirondack chair
Sunk into the pebbled shore of Yuba.
That morning was misty and my wool blanket
  Held water droplets on its fibers in petite constellations.
  Beneath my feet on the slippery rocks,
I watched caddisfly larvae gathering stones
And eating the algae beneath the fresh water,
Ignoring the pink smoke that paraded like camels
Across the sky, hiding the morning star,
In the thick morning air that covered our shoulders
It felt like my husband's heavy linen jacket
Still warm from his body --
I breathed and my tongue was on fire
Memories of the burning steel bins we set
Behind the hardware store and away from the streets
That were buzzing with taxis, women, feet;
I stared at the blank sky, far away and crackling
To get my mind off of my blinking.
How delightfully naive it was so long ago
          To drill into my Girl Scout troop
The names of constellations
          We would never be able to find.

The Avocado tree in Lawndale

What an unlikely place to have a tree,
Especially this: a fruit tree matured
Into harvest, though with no guarantee
The avocados, through winter, be spared.

I was never worried about the yield
Until I moved out into my own debut;
Alone, I went grocery shopping and held
A hardened stone fruit in an strange milieu.

This fruit was not suspended on a branch,
Also adored from the kitchen window
For months, watching it grow verdant and match
The late afternoon suburban shadow.

Nor had it spent weekends being breathed on
By little girls hiding from goblins who
Chased them into the sanctuary swan
Wings of her who felt their skin rise and fall.

The hard fruit stranger sat dark in my hand
An avocado I had never met.

The Sex Life of Trees

The rumor is that the air was thick
In the beginning.

As it is during any
Honeymoon period.

The air was full of breaths
That hung in the boughs
Like time suspended in the arms
All along the slender body of the silk tree
That stood along the perimeter of the grove
In her spun gown that flashed pink in the afternoon —

The breaths were hot,
Surging with life, and
Stifling —

In the beginning there were plants.
Large plants, small plants, spiny plants,
Leggy plants, busty plants,
plants with spindly fingers
Plants with eyes underground,
Plants with cauliflower ears above;
Green plants, sexy plants, plants that
Give it up all day, and plants that
Were so loud
You couldn't miss them.

The Sibyl trees could see over them all,
Past any gate;
past the four rivers that
Divided the land into purposes
Of gold, onyx;
They would raise the canopy to see farther
Than even the present,
Some, blasphemously, said they could see
Past the umbra of the day.
The trees ruled as the aristocracy
Due to their given gifts of intellectual
And, I suppose, moral superiority.

There was a clamorous planet of plants,
They lived beneath the canopy of trees.

The rumor was,

between friends,
After Penemue wrote down all their names
And promised to call them later,
It was the roots of the trees
That crawled underneath the brush
And touched each other under the covers
Of the lowest layer of our form;
When all formation was said and done,

It was the trees
who got out of bed, first;
Whose names we have forgotten.

Part II

Shame

Reds-Greens-Browns

I remember
One time, in 2018, there was an evening when I was studying
By myself in a restaurant hidden in the back of some bohemian alley
In the crook of downtown, forgotten
By the neon signs lining the street and advertising
For drinks that could be found inside,
Like Corona or Budweisser. Common drinks that feel
Familiar. They feel like the memory of drinking beer
With your hilariously vulgar uncle in the backyard when your parents
Couldn't see you taking small sips of the horrible beverage
And trying to mask the smell from your breath at dinner
By chewing on tomato leaves from your mother's raised garden.
It was a nice table I was at.
I was finishing my graduate degree, after dropping out when I was twenty-six.
I was pregnant with my second that year, and I could not, for the life
Of me, remember what I was reading that semester. That's fine.
I came back to it later. I was turning forty that month.
It was a nice table.
It is a nice memory. One that should smell
Like garlic bread and Chardin's Eau de Cologne.
With my work laid out like a sacrificial lamb I sat
in this outdoor patio restaurant,
Underneath thin green strings of tiny lightbulbs,
Which was a nice feel —
The light felt soft, like a kitchen ceiling light
Stained by years of steam that erupted
Out of my grandmother's stock pot —
And enjoying a mug of wine; also so bohemian;
On my own terms. With my own company and ordering my own
Food and sipping my bohemian wine and listening to
A family next to me, the whole thing.
There was a grandmother speaking rapidly
In Portugese and the little boy whining for more bread before his dinner arrived,
And the parents shifting silverware around
While an older man — he was loud like an uncle —
Was complaining about the neighbors who kept parking
Their car in front of his house, probably (obviously) on purpose,
And the baby on an older woman's lap
Chewing on a blanket, oblivious
To the older woman's overwhelming perfume
She used to hide the thinning of her hairline or
To distract a man, a mature single man, from the yellowing of her skin.
The mesh table was draped with a longwhite linen cloth
Catching the breadcrumbs of the little boy and
The hand gestures of the uncle and the little splash of wine

That escaped from the young mother's glass as she set it down
A little too quickly, revealing her annoyance at this ceasless
banter on her one night out this week —

I was trying to cut back on drinking because I remebered not remembering
The end of the night the week before when I went out with a girlfriend
And we went out drinking like we had just invented feminism
And we just got our voting cards and we were allowed into the University library
Unchaperoned and we laughed at the pigeons and we drank
Vodka martinis and the bus ride should have smelled like
Cigarettes and feet but I couldn't remember smelling
Even that, let alone how I got home and in bed safely;
I avoided vodka, that night, at the bohemian cafe.
I waited for my small meal of pasta to arrive and I drank wine,
Whatever red blend they had on the menu,
Like I was a young college girl who was out for the night after
Borrowing my parents' car and I had a curfew.
In between breaths, I noticed
Beside me were three tomato baskets,
Holding back well-tended, tall cherry tomato
Plants, one can only imagine to inspire
The eater to eat more.

I touched the leaf, well within reach.
And I was ashamed, right there in front
Of the grandmother, the child, the
Parents, the black sky, God behind
The stars,
That I could not smell the leaf.
I held it in between my fingers,
As if it was something more than a leaf,
That it was a memory of my mother's garden
That had been tilled and covered with a concrete patio, long ago;

I could never smell any of these things.
The garlic bread, the Chardin's Eau de Cologne, the wine
In the mug, the family sitting next to me, the tomato leaf.

Because my head had been broken
A long, long time ago. It was a car. I was outside the car.
I don't remember being there. But I remember that
My face had been reconstructed.
My leg had pins and screws holding myself together.
My skull had healed; mostly. There are dips in the bone, here and there.
I remember when my eye was a little more firm to the touch.
The memory of the event was fuzzy.
And, when I held the tomato leaf, I could never really remember
How I ever could smell.

Bee Eaters

For Lake Quinault

Our feet were surrounded by clovers,
Dotting the sloped lawns
Like a Georges Seurat painting,
Smelling like sunscreen.
Feet, dozens of them, moved
Across the greens, touching the clovers,
Playing horseshoes with friends
Whose hands threw the shoes
Like a frisbee, rather than like
Their grandfathers' who tossed
A gentle underhand swing.
These grandfathers knew how to win.
They kept their boat shoes on
When they played, their form
Was stiff and loose -
They played with the wind because
They have felt the wind before.
It was June, the season of lotus blossoms,
When we were all paying
Our sights to the dangers we
Could see, like drowning in the lake,
Or getting lost looking for the restroom;

We would not notice the bees
On the clovers, near the horseshoes.

The Lonely Moon

When I plan my grocery list,
There is an order.
Because I was the oldest child
And was in charge of cooking;
Because I was desperate for friends
And hosted dinner-parties;
Because I have a large family
And we need food.

—

There are lists.
Lists of meal times, lists of
Meals, lists of items
For meals.

—

Typically, I order the items
On the page by aisle.
This saves time in the store
So I do not get stuck on aisle 5
Second-guessing what I had gotten
And what I missed.

—

So, when the year of restraint
Descended on my life of order
Like a plague of biting uncertainty
And failure —

You see, as the oldest child, as
A people-pleaser, as a nervous
Adult, as a Strong American Woman —

I hate to fail.

It is the worst feeling while you are
Still alive.

I hate to fail.

And it is everywhere in my life.

I have failed to live up to my potential,
Whatever that means;
I have failed Trigonometry,
No love lost there;
I have failed to earn my mother's love -
That was a fool's errand;
I have failed my religious journey,
According to churches I have attended
(According to the members
In the churches I have attended);
I have failed to take my vitamins every morning;
I have failed to love myself as I love others;
I have failed my driver's test, twice;
I have failed the real estate exam, once;
I have failed to learn how to meditate correctly;
I have failed to be in the now, or do my laundry
On time, or finish *Moby Dick,* or write a novel,
Or win any awards, or run a mile, or
Keep a garden growing.

And the reverberations of these failures,
I have to assume, led to the world
Shutting down.

—

I wasn't allowed in the grocery store.
No one was.
(Except for the "essential workers" who
Definitely got the short stick of gratitude)

—

I failed to keep the order
Of my lists.

Insecurity of my worth was just the beginning.

But, I adapted.

I figured out how to order
Order
Groceries online.

They were delivered to my porch
By heavily gloved and masked women.

We waved to each other

Through my window.

—

In those days that turned into years
Of restraint,
I victoriously discovered new flaws in myself.

I do not read the fine print
So carefully as it requires.

Such is life: it is simple
Until it is not.

In life, you live and breathe
Until you don't.

It's that simple.
For the most part.

—

I ordered boxes of cereal
Only to have delivered on my porch

Boxes and boxes and boxes of cereal:
The one item was a 4-pack.

Or heads and heads and heads of broccoli,
And cans and cans and cans of soup,
Or stalks and stalks and stalks of celery,
And boxes and boxes and boxes of broth.

—

It all adds up.
The cans, the boxes, the heads,
The fine print, the misreadings,
The lists, the orders, the processes,
The failures, the shames, the stone
In my throat that protrude in public out
Of my natural shape so everyone
Can obviously see how
I am imperfect.

—

When I see the moon during the day,

Being out of order of the day,
And I remember that it is a reflection
Of the object in space
That is also reflecting the light
From somewhere else
Because it is a people-pleaser
That is desperate for friends in the night
Even though it cannot create light
On its own.

The words unspoken and written in bubbles:
A, B.

A, B.

Nervous?

It is quite possible,
Very possible

That you were born a porcupine
Merely reincarnated

And in your past life you were not
So young

While you navigated the old waters of
The river

And listened to Porter or Gershwin
All night

While watching the blood pills
Roll around

In the bottom of the whiskey glass —
Old man.

For the record nothing is forbidden
Out right

And yet — the inches we keep between
Our glasses

Are syllables of intention
Unsaid schemes

Admitting the insecurity we, I, crafted
Back when

I said so what and took on all that
Was possible —

The words unspoken and written in bubbles:
A, B.

The Propeller

I couldn't tell you how big, ghastly large
The propeller looked underneath the salt
Water which cushioned the ship
In the harbor.

It was bigger than my breasts who stood
Next to me and admired the red metal gears.
It was too big.

Even the ship felt too big, just floating
There beside the pier like a body in a bathtub,
Bobbing and splashing water into the overflow hole.

There was too much of it to stomach, for me.
My breasts wanted to stay, boyant,
but I ran out of the room and hid
behind the iron pipes nearby -

My Jungian shadow slinking out to find me.

I remember leaving the ship with my body in tow;
I never returned. Why would I?
I can see the propeller in my mind
That was bigger than my mouth which was open
And unspeaking as I drove away
With this ghastly large memory.

Dear Enemy

My enemy was there.
I was there.
I rolled my bicycle roots out into the street
Beyond the reaching roots of the banyan,
Across the submerged system of the sequoias,
Into the valley at the precipice of black walnut trees
Black vulcanized tires; we were there.
Yes, I was there.

That day, I remember watching the clouds
Playing out the film of my life
In crisp white puffs across the blue screen.
We were together on that street,
My enemy and I.

—

I remember that day, even though
It didn't matter.
Does it matter what day it was?
It was a weekday, because I was leaving school.
Who was my enemy, before
That day?
I had no enemies.
I was too young for enemies.
I did not know any enemies, not real enemies
That steal your babies or plunder
The house while the family is out at the movies.
I did not know the darlings who
Dawdle, who appear; on the street.
Their shadows are in the sunlight like
Stones in my stomach;
To tiptoe into my territory —

My home where I grew my children
And where I fed them, at noon,
Goldfish and apple juice
And watched them race all over
The forest floor that smelled like
tar and tasted wild —

I could hear their voice at the door,
And I would recognize my enemy:
Wouldn't I?

—

Was the sun my enemy? Were the birds
Which sung in the morning and in the dusk
My enemy?
Who was my enemy?

I recognize
My enemy
When
I
Was
There.

—

My memories are with my enemy;
My friend, who I knew.
My feet remember touching the bark
My toes balancing on the wheels
My eyes remember the clouds
That were telling my story
On the blue screen
Drifting in the sky
Above the magnolia trees
That were tucked in the sidewalk
That shaded the children
That.

—

The blonde petals.
The me.
The enemy.

—

What appearance would we recognize
As an enemy?

People do not walk around the world with
"Enemy"
Taped to their foreheads.

—

My dear enemy lives in the space
Which belongs to them

And which belongs to me.
My enemy is there.
I am there.

—

My dear enemy lives in the moment
The scene,
The impact.

In the neighborhood with the neighbor
Who turned them in.

That is the plot point when we say,
When we remember,
The moment
And say, "Ah, yes,
This is my enemy:
The figure who looks like a friend."

SVT

Then --
-- It stops.
A signature --
Mark the time,
10:36 p.m.
A rock,
A pound,
A bag of shifting sand
Sliding in the pericardium
Dropping in rhythmic clumps
And I mark the time:
My life, beat.
Beat, halt --
Beat.

Pastoral of Love

Easy to say I didn't know;
        Who does?
They were wasps,
We found them outside after hitting
The stump that stood at the brim of the forest,
That stung me and my children
And followed us home and into
The bathroom where we
Hit the air and the walls, wild
Aegis flying around our faces;
Our eyes were open and we could see
The wasps dart and sing all of our skins
And it hurt and we all hurt together,
And we hurt in silence because
We dared not open our mouths
Lest the winged monsters found
Our weakness and could get inside
Where it is darkest and they would
Flutter their way through our guts
By echolocation and screams and
We would feel the beat of their wings
Hit bones, and we would beat ourselves
To try to crush them from the outside.
I didn't know where the wasp nest was;
        Otherwise, I would have gone around.

Coterie

The very nature of drowning requires:
to death.

This thought
was only
a couple of minutes.

The causation
of the water is,

was,

there between
Between the clefts of the splitting land

which divided
people who stood

on the land and who grasped
onto roots as the land

split

and

as the divide

widened

and

the water rose
from the depth which
we did not know

was there, and we,

had the earth —

for a moment.

Shorter than the breath we held.

The Snail

What else could a feather do
But fall?

Like the wet sand into the
Littoral space.

Like spiderwebs into
The wind;

Like the snails who fought
In Medieval tapestries,

They melteth away
Like slime in the wash,

As the wooden bucket into the well after
The deluge.

Lost in the 80s

At some point, it was 5:46pm on Friday.
We were so close to being done with the week.
Long ago, someone down the street drove off,
Skipping out on the weekend ceremony.
We played games in the 80s, together;
No one lost in the 80s. We were all winners.
The first storm clouds roll in from ElSegundo,
And I am 7 years old, watching TV with my grandparents.
There is coarsely chopped iceberg salad laid
in a thin wooden bowl with Thousand Island Dressing.
We, who sat in the living room, lived
When I was 7 years old. We, who breathed the
LosAngeles air, thick as blood,
And glowing pink against the clouds.
I am sitting on a maroon corduroy sofa, and we,
Who are all watching television with our necks turned.
There were word-puzzles on the screen; I could never guess
what the words were going to become:
 I was only 7, after all. I knew how to spell
 My name, my address, and the President.
The rain blew the magnolia trees outside with a transposal of
the sea:
 It was cold outside, and my family was anemic.
 Our warmth was pumped through slats in the wooden floor,
We, who were alive to breathe and win games,
When I was 7 years old in the living room.
Pat Sajak makes the final call
as the waves lap the windows.
And we all win.
It was the 80s,
When we were we.

Penumbra Deosculation

*and other words that a poetry professor one told me that normal
people don't use in daily life.*

My written disclosure was clumsy and did not
Come easily; naturally, none do.
My fingers could form the awkward words,
In bits and stones and drips.
None of them came out of my mouth
Like locusts.
I am sure, nearly positive,
That these words were alive
Because I could smell them
Burning and lingering like tinder from the woods,
Wandering between boughs of a house tree
And thumping, darkly,
Sounding like the sacrificial doves
That will not yet die
Until the words are spoken above them
With weight and with wait,
Until their smell burned with feathers still beating
Words that people don't normally use in daily life.

The Volta

The OED added besmite to its
Longform prose;
Burroughs murdered his wife;
I guess we've moved on.

What haven't we named.

In the eternity of 15 minutes,
What do we have left.

Maybe we should finally name
Cheese on toast.

We could start at the beginning,
When we learned how to name
Through touching and verse:

If the world was a literary trope,
A poem the length of the universe which
Drafted life into the pages, delivering
An ode of breath exhuming the aubade
Drawing clouds which rise in an iambic apex,
Lines upon lines enjambed into the next,
Showing with words the wind over the face
Of the waters and the burst of
A voice which spoke the sun
Into existing, lines which flicked the cricket
Into motion, enjambed to released gates
Of the waters, into forming the behemoth
Within the quatrain of the earth, to whispering
Lyrical diction into the ears of the
Eagles, to whistling an old melody
Into the boughs of cedars, to riding
The waves of Joppa and singing
With the leviathan beneath emanations'
foot, to shining a glint in the corner
Of the coyote's eye as it recognized
Its purpose beside the hare, to the
Rock which lay in wait for the rhythmic
Blow of the chisel to procure the
Metal from its vein, to the fires which
Galvanized the swords and
hung from the hips of men marching
along the crimson *adamah*, beating
the grass into roads and raising their fists

as if to imitate the swing
Of the heavens in a wide, rain-specked
Arc across the sky -

Was the volta,
The harsh movement when my violent cough
Dislodged the stone pit
Lodged so firmly in my throat, silently
Welling up inflamed words
Which had dripped down into a pool
Of swampy feelings, and suddenly

Named a verb.

Searching for the body in the wood

For Sebastian

We searched for the dog on Sunday,
All of us whistling
Three notes, ones that
The dog might recognize.
My daughter wore my
Gray sweatpants,
Thinking maybe the dog
Would recognize them
And return home away
From these woods filled
With ivy
And
Coyotes.
Least of all, I try
Not to think
Of the howls
Which remind
Us while we lay
Half asleep in our beds
How close
They are.

The icon that is not California, at all

Now, the icon of my past fades
Since it is in the past and since
I have let my love for the land
Bleed out, all along.

Appellation, *Icon*, in error
Due to the granite fact
That it, *California*, exists
Outside of my memory bank.
Which is awkward.

It feels like my childhood is crafted
In postcards orbiting my judgement
Flashing pictures I recognize
And tack on necessary sensory
Attributes to flesh it out.

I tack on the smell of dry grass
That baked like bricks every summer,
Or the smell of chlorinated city water
Out of the warm, pliable hose;
The Yuba river with its unbearably
Cold water from the dwindling snow pack;
The ancient mountain houses
Hidden in the Sierras.
I knew the names of every plant:
Golden yarrow, basket grass, foxtail.
I knew where to find the golden trout
Ten thousand feet above sea-level.

Icons, silent and dimming,
A sobriquet I named myself,
As if these sunbleached pictures
Which fade into golden hues
Justifies the absurd attachment I had.
Even though, truthfully, I know
it was an empty fidelity to a land
Of dirt and rocks and water,
which didn't know me;
But, also, never refused my touch.

Part III

Self

The Word for Her

Verbum, which actually starts with
The wuh sound, is a word for word.

How marvelous to hear a word
And see it as a word.

The Buffalo Run

I caused a stampede
A long time ago

After she wouldn't pick
Up the phone, or

Wouldn't listen to the
Words I wrote down

On store-bought cards
Covered in glitter butterflies,

I honked the horn of my car
And caused a stampede in the hills;

And I watched the cows run
When I could not run.

————

Iron, my mother tongue,
Dyes seasoned in fire,

Spit across hands
Splayed like a bird

On the walls only
To be covered entirely

By red iron pigments,
And preserved in caves,

Found later by archeologists
Who marveled at, understandably,

How the trees were preserved
For eternity as if a stone,

And how the buffalo ran across the stone walls
Without running.

Singularity

I kept my crystal glass
Half full of gin and juniper tonic —

And we'll answer that pestering argument:
The glass is full of gin and tonic
And the empty space is full
Of nothing
except time.

So,
I kept the glass half full
In order to keep
Myself from
Drinking wine, too.

Because that's the problem
With people —

You can fill your glass with too many peoples
Until you get very, very drunk
And hate drinking entirely.

Somewhere on a hill of white pebbles

Are birds still holding out
for the phenomenon of life subject to
the natural law —

it is so hard to say
yet their arboreal sway was indisputably
aspirational,
until the trees disappeared.

And then —

Somewhere on a hill of white pebbles,
Next to the garden hose which ran for eternity,
In the corner of a dead crabgrass lawn
At the edge of Lawndale where a barley farm once grew
In which still nests my first lost tooth
Which landed there after Cheryl slapped my mouth,
Near a stump that used to be a magnolia tree,

Named after the Osage Nation which lived
2,062 miles away from this hill of white pebbles
In the heart of Lawndale, sister to Compton
As the crow flew from tree to tree and dropped
filbert nuts

Onto the dark tar roads as I watched them
With my eyes low against the ground
Dance on the asphalt, change in the heat,
The low 6 inches of unsteady horizon —

A keyhole in the trees
Subject to law.

Cocktails on the water

His elbow held me.
That was how I knew it was love.

The Definition of Manslaughter

I really have to do something
About all these oranges.
I bought a whole damn box of them,
With grand intensions of eating.

There might be 25, or 30,
Sitting like Svengali in the wires,
Staring at me while I spread marmalade onto toast;

Withered expressions, all of them.
Waiting to die in the afternoon.

Who really knows, about simple fruits.
They have the same color as the swimming fish
Of anamensis, stirring the pot,
Tap, tapping parts of yesterday for food,
For voices I remember, a song I heard
On the radio, wondering how to spell
Boudoir correctly - is there a silent x? -
Or is that *Bordeaux.*

My heart skips, as it does.
Some nameless heart condition.
Not fatal, I'm told; well, eventually.

I take a bite of orange — A sip of water.

What do I know about sin;
It was grown on the tree.
I didn't put it there.
The fruit had risen, risen up, and fell;

A shortcoming of valor, risen in stature.
A staple in children's books.

I feel it in the crease of my nose, the sin,
the memories, rising inside and
Peeling my wrinkled, fearless skin apart in strips
Leaving stretch marks like a map
Stretched thin across the north Atlantic

Driving women to the market,
Listening to the song the orchards have forgotten;

I walk my fingers across the map,
Tip toe, tip toe along the dotted lines.

The oranges sting underneath the nail;
The peel, the flesh, the thin juice.
I pick the flesh out of my fingers.
There are just so many to go through.

Shorf View, and other misleading signs in life

In the forest, you quickly learn how
To walk undisturbed
In the rain, followed
By the lesson of missing the hour
Of sun when the clouds break.
These are the lessons you learn out here.

And that is where I found myself —
Hardly in a metaphysical sense,
Even being in a forest and tempted
By transcendental mischiefs —
Since I could finally see the sun today,
I was, undoubtably, outside.

———————

It was Monday.
It was an uneventful walk.
Across the Sound was a postcard picture
Of Seattle, sitting quietly in the foreground
Of the Cascade mountains crisp with snow.
I passed typical 3-bedroom houses
Whose yards were overwhelmed with spring,
Bursting forth with both life
And *Danger: No Trespassing* signs on every fence.
It seemed understandable, as I walked along:
Persons who choose to live on islands
Tend to be more concerned
With both consecrated privacy, and also
With how many leagues lie between
Them and crime they read about in the news.

———————

At the end of the road,
At the vista point which gazed south
Across the nearly pelagic ferry route,
I stood on an ivy-bursting cliff,
Behind a copse of trees,
Overlooking a small harbor
With a significantly low tide
Which allowed islanders
to walk where water once stood;
Perhaps trying to will the event into reality
(*Who knows*)

I stood next to a sign where it was written:
Shorf View,
Which is exactly how I pronounced it, out loud,
Because I impulsively wondered with electricity
If a Shorf was a special type
Of dangerous cliff unique only to this island,
Which could possibly account for the numerous
Danger signs I passed
On the way here while walking
Through a very quiet, empty, rural neighborhood
And didn't even consider
The bolt which affixed the sign to the post
Being placed on the bottom of the *E*
Until I thought about it, later.

Prizes

Even though it is a thing
        Offered as a reward

To the person who excelled
        In some outstanding way —

It was easy to mistake the vernacular
        Of heresy as a common

Tenet rather than
        Something more particular,

Like a grafted tree
        Or a wild gourd.

Ten-Dollar Word

I remember,
When my dying aunt asked for us

to stop putting cut flowers
Around her bed;

The smells
Were keeping her awake.

Part IV

Hope

Ode to a Green Beetle on the Chicken Coop

Long, long were the green antenna
That sprung out of its head

Like lovers wires and phosphorus fires
Foretelling future's spread.

The beetle lay between the sheaths
Of scratch board and of glue

It arched its shadow between the panes
Of glossy morning dew.

I found its verdant sheen reflect
Against the window panes

Which once housed violent beaks I owned
Who lived within these frames.

The gash in wood beneath the bug
I traced with my eye.

A larger creature came for them
As the stars clung to the sky.

Beauty creeps on spindly legs
I watch as it steps on.

When once there might have death been here,
The beetle carries on.

Aubade as Mushrooms

No, it isn't the most natural thing;
It doesn't feel so natural to me,
To love a thing that grows so low to the earth;

I thought love would be an ethereal
Thing, brought down by twinkling Celtic fairies
Sprinkling love dust into floral hearts

Sniffed by lovers who succumb to their wiles,
And willingly carried away in gales
Of magical fairy dust that means love.

How was I to know, love would grow so slow,
Down below the garden gate, below stems,
Down, down underneath the lowest violet,

I never thought to look beneath our toes
Where mushrooms grow so slow, as
Shadows that creep over, across and down

Drainpipes or fenceposts, through compost and moss;
Inverted holes that capture the dew in
Hills, away from the things of magic.

Love, slow love, love that I found nestled deep
In these earthly vessels, lying so low
And growing with mushrooms as slow as the air.

No, it isn't the most natural thing
To look for love on the earth, with my hands;
Yet, there I found your smile, creeping slowly
In the shadows of the fenceposts, and we grew
A slow love between our fingers and toes.

The Sense of Movement

On Sunday, I finally decided
To try oat milk in my coffee,
After years of listening to advertisements,
Friends, and siblings declare allegiance.

I have never had an issue with cow's milk,
Nor have I had the habit of adding milk
To my coffee, nor do I eat cereal, nor
Have I thought too long about my own milk-fidelity.

Nevertheless, it feels like times are moving.
In the store, I notice more alternatives
Drawing people away from what we grew up with.
What we expect to be the accepted.

Maybe the cows might need a breather;
Maybe the orchards are eager to lean in;

Or perhaps it is we who are eager to see a change
Of color across the aisles,
As we are eager to see blossoms on the trees
Bursting in prom-pink at the cusp of spring.

Hydrants

After the 80s, there weren't many occasions
When fire hydrants were opened
Just to let the inner city children
Have some reprieve from the unrelenting
Freedom and liberty of summer.

I remember watching the news cover
These fire hydrant events with the same
Steady cam shots zooming in on
Bare-chested boys jumping into
The core of the torrent as if they
Were fighting against the very nature
Of childhood and beating it back with
Wide eyes and glistening teeth completely
Unaware of oncoming cars or cameras
Watching their every move —

I suppose the reporter stayed a little longer
In order to remind the audience of
The times in our lives when water,
Just the feeling of water on our skin,
Or the thrust of water pushing us over,
Or the earthly smell of water fresh
Out of the pipes,
Could buoy the weight of other memories,
Like returning to our homes in the middle of summer
And making sure the key was still
In the little mesh pocket inside our trunks.

By the knuckle of my thumb

I may be
the kind of person
Who enjoys attention, although
If I want to be truthful,
Which is as difficult as
Sifting horsehairs
Out of a box of violin strings;
I enjoy the vanity of participating
To the point of leading.

Case in point -
I participated in my childhood
By observing myself.
There were magical moments
In wildflower fields that had
Created a perimeter surrounding me;
Then, being a child and solipsist.

And then, when the solipsism wore off
And I was in charge of adult things
Like feelings and rent and consequences,
I, once, held a peach that I
Had bought with my own money,
in the peak peach season,
And I gently pressed my thumb into its flesh,
And I ate it until it became me.

Chevrolets

And then, a night swallowed me:
In the cool seaside draft it felt
The driftwood fire of the bourgeoisie,
Eating marine and sandy veldt.

In its flushed moon face, the foreshore lode
Reflected blush from the flowering tree:
The tides driven back —buffaloed —
Caravans of Calliopes.

I would have liked to curl up on his tongue
Until ante night descended
Low, in clumps of sand where gray crabs clung —
My heavy eyes, eventide, suspended.

But I tire, and our children
Sleep inside, deaf to mouths of night
Guided by the moon, which again
Slips in ebb, a tide, a satellite.

The opal flames of sunrise reveals
Quondam hours through bygone days,
Flashed upon the dark waves of wheels:
Nights of coffee and Chevrolets.

Love in Tomato Fields

It is like what I imagine love to be:
Dark. Hovering over the chaos
Like September fog floating over tomato fields
Stroking the leaves as they sleep;
And I slept next to them.

I was alive, according to the sun.
And I was in love, according to the night.

I would watch the sun rise
With company
in the tomato field next to the service road.

The Summerhouse

My haughty disrespect for the foundations of astronomy
means nothing to my guiltless soul;
Into thin and spindly shadows my tongue lies,
moved by the absence of light.

And I have no interest in tasting the drug of Nyx.
Mixing dark potions together to create day,
Or seducing a hidden tongue to sing
Words into life.
This light, these words which cling to my lips;
It lounges on my chair and sneaks up to my face until
It catches my eye and I confess:
"We were lovers, yes?"

I taste in enslaving licks of lights
breathed onto my head, fanning the shadeless tooth,
animating the brilliant vermillion beneath;
I feel the aureate words wrestle

in my mouth;
The turgid prose fills the cavities
across my tongue and I am rich -
I stash pennies under my tongue.

 I struggle like a fool with the words.
No gleaming firelight, nor simple oil lamp
has spoken to me, restoring life to my bones

Like poetry.
Crystal'd, selfish starlit skies have taken
far too many hot breaths from my lips;
My sight is gone, my tongue is hot.

Ethereal divides divulging the least effulgence
As food, as smoke: a cluster of tiny prima donnas
suspended above the waters.

Far away.

Far, far away and silent,
having put all of their minotaurs to sleep,
Deep, deep in the heart of the city,
In the space of a line,
In the pause.

I lick my lip.
And yet…and still! The golden string uncoils,
glistening between my thighs as I walk,
Across the face of the oil which suspends
This language, these words which
Wail -
Like ravens chasing an owl.

It is, the words, my words,
set apart in the span of days
I had never lived through, but which
have been written by the fulgent feathered quill:

The seduction, the arrogant allure
of the language I need to recognize,
As kin, as a lover, as my own flesh,
The words burn sulphur into my hands,
Spits fire into my eyes and,
Demanding, moves my mouth: It,
which sits like a whore on the page.
I read.
I read. The Summerhouse

My haughty disrespect for the foundations of astronomy
means nothing to my guiltless soul;
Into thin and spindly shadows my tongue lies,
moved by the absence of light.

And I have no interest in tasting the drug of Nyx.
Mixing dark potions together to create day,
Or seducing a hidden tongue to sing
Words into life.
This light, these words which cling to my lips;
It lounges on my chair and sneaks up to my face until
It catches my eye and I confess:
"We were lovers, yes?"

I taste in enslaving licks of lights
breathed onto my head, fanning the shadeless tocth,
animating the brilliant vermillion beneath;
I feel the aureate words wrestle

in my mouth;
The turgid prose fills the cavities
across my tongue and I am rich -

I stash pennies under my tongue.

I struggle like a fool with the words.

No gleaming firelight, nor simple oil lamp
has spoken to me, restoring life to my bones

Like poetry.
Crystal'd, selfish starlit skies have taken
far too many hot breaths from my lips;
My sight is gone, my tongue is hot.

Ethereal divides divulging the least effulgence
As food, as smoke: a cluster of tiny prima donnas
suspended above the waters.

Far away.

Far, far away and silent,
having put all of their minotaurs to sleep,
Deep, deep in the heart of the city,
In the space of a line,
In the pause.

I lick my lip.
And yet...and still! The golden string uncoils,
glistening between my thighs as I walk,
Across the face of the oil which suspends
This language, these words which
Wail -
Like ravens chasing an owl.

It is, the words, my words,
set apart in the span of days
I had never lived through, but which
have been written by the fulgent feathered quill:

The seduction, the arrogant allure
of the language I need to recognize,
As kin, as a lover, as my own flesh,
The words burn sulphur into my hands,
Spits fire into my eyes and,
Demanding, moves my mouth: It,
which sits like a whore on the page.
I read.
I read.

Dove Feathers

It isn't a confession which
Comes easily; naturally, none do.

My mouth could form the words,
If only I could remember what for.

I am sure, nearly positive,
There is something, perhaps are,

Which threaten the sanctity of me;
Some piece, consecrated, for someone.

It nags, as an itchy bag of wheat,
And it thumps, somewhere.

It is as if the sacrificial doves
Have not yet died, and they still breathe on my neck.

The fat has not been burnt, nor
Has the priest taken down my name.

My mind turns on the spit, as if
There was something left over;

Something I left somewhere.
Someone I forgot.

Waking Up With Virginia

Our mother, Virginia Woolf:
have we all barricaded ourselves
Inside our rooms of distractions? These words,
These images creating this contained room,
which once brought so much joy to the heart,
To the bosom of the woman in whose
White-knuckled hand held the instrument of ink
Which would splash down, quietly;
These words whose *différance* trace
To the blank page on the desk above the Thames
And instructed the feminine self to write,
To build a new creation, to give birth
To a word;
One black stroke,
After another.

We, I, have surrounded ourselves, myself, with film;
Screens, filters, and our march of ribbons.
Purpose — what is the meaning of life? —
Is muffled by sensible
Rubber-soled shoes which do not slip
Across the splash of tile;
So we do not curse in front of our guests.

Perhaps I saw you, myself, in the over-arched lobby
When I drove by;
Clad in lapels and wool.
Silently nodding off as we,
The mighty, the feminine,
Fought to allow these screens
To use our profile
When we buy the book online, anyway.
No one to argue with at the register
About refusing membership to the store,
And whatnot.

Your shadow loomed across my fingers
When I got distracted. A million voices —
Or maybe a dozen — piling up on my desk
As one collected voice, and I cannot distinguish
My own from the stack of papers anymore;
The hours and hours of reading others' voices
And scrunching up my face to empathize —
Silently, mind you —
With the marks on the screen;

The marks, one after another, building words
That might be from another woman,
But we really will never know, and it doesn't matter
One way or another, because I couldn't hear your voice
In the pile of scraps of paper because,
At the edge of the page, where the words were
Cut off:
I ended up —
I'll say it; buying a dress online.

There was still a tab open
For the library, which would not let you in,
Which launched the line of ebooks;
So I could read your tireless crusade
In the peace of my kitchen,
With no witnesses.
No congregation.

I am sold protein bars and yogurts
in the margins;
To help with my weight and digestion —
How did you ever deal with irregularity?
It seems to be the only topic of polite
Conversation left to us.
Even the weather has turned.

About the Author

Tamarah Rockwood graduated from Harvard with an ALM in Creative Writing and Literature in 2020 and has had many publications including short stories, screenwriting, and poetry in the University of Canberra Vice Chancellor's International Poetry Prize, among other published poetry. She is the CEO of Bainbridge Island Press's publishing house, which publishes poetry chapbooks, collections, and anthologies. She is the manager of Ars Poetica in Washington state. Other than writing, she was the former Wine Committee Chairwoman for the Rainier Club in Seattle; now the current Literary Committee Chairwoman. Along with living the literary life, she tends a small plump of ducks on Bainbridge Island with her husband of 20+ years, Ben, and their 5 children. She enjoys reading literature, she does not enjoy reading YA literature, she is in love with 1930-1950 movies on TCM, and, despite living in a PNW forest, she is not keen on hiking.

www.ingramcontent.com/pod-product-compliance
Lightning Source LLC
Chambersburg PA
CBHW051641120626
46551CB00014B/2171